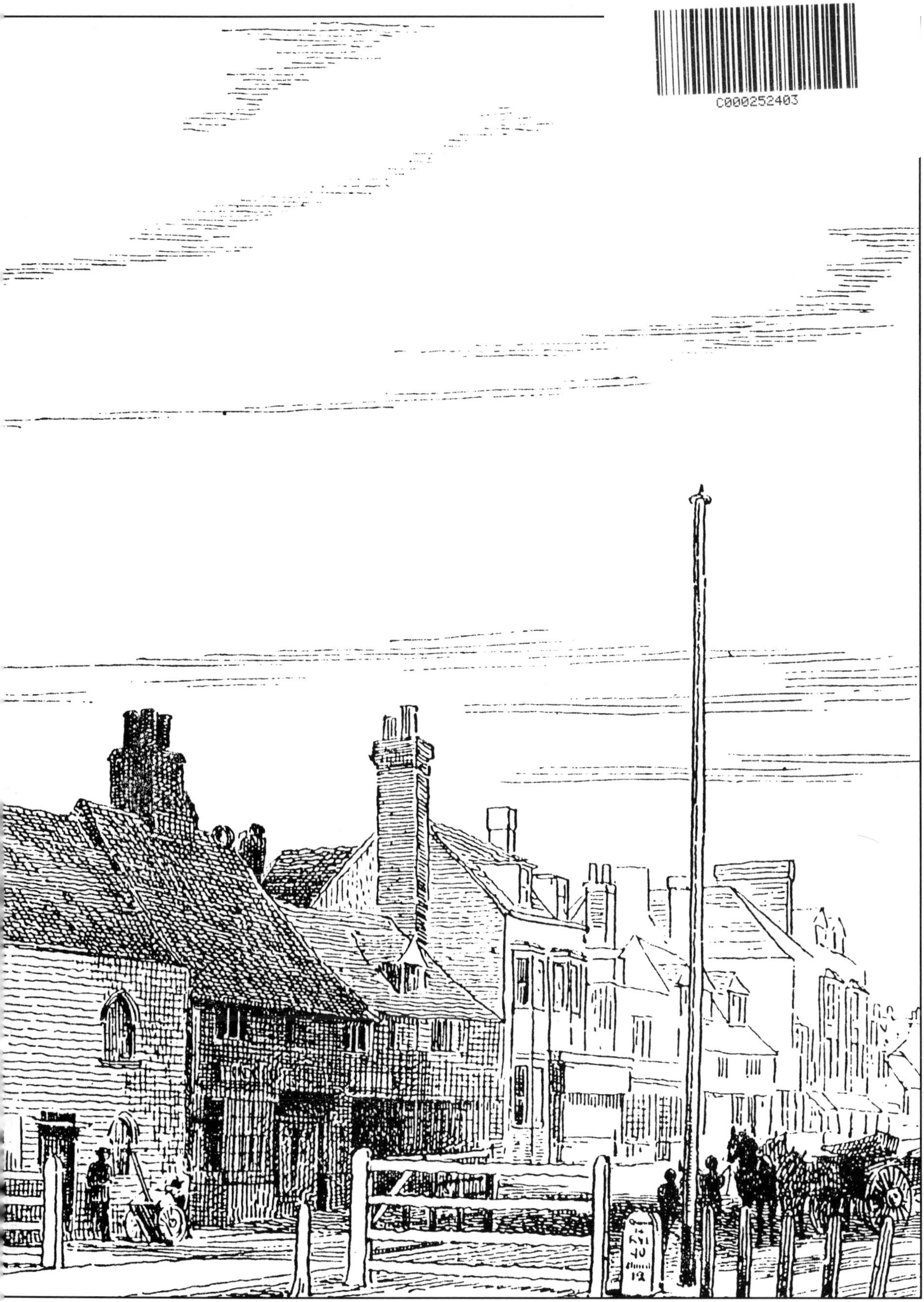

BYGONE
TENTERDEN

Bells Lane, Tenterden.

BYGONE
TENTERDEN

Aylwin Guilmant

Phillimore

1991

Published by
PHILLIMORE & CO. LTD.
Shopwyke Hall, Chichester, Sussex

ISBN 0 85033 785 2

Printed and bound in Great Britain by
BIDDLES LTD.
Guildford, Surrey

This book is dedicated to
all those people who love Tenterden

List of Illustrations

Frontispiece: Bells Lane, Tenterden

Smallhythe

Acknowledgements

I would like to thank the following for their permission to use certain of their photographs and other relevant material, particularly the books and documents which are the property of Tenterden Town Council: Ms. Stella Bellem, Curator of the Museum of Kent Rural Life; Mrs. C. Bottrill, Tenterden Town Clerk; Councillor Stuart G. Brown; Dr. D. B. G. Burgess, Administrator of Tenterden Museum; Ms. Christine Dunn and other members of staff at Kent County Library in Maidstone; Mr. Yinnon Ezra, Director of Art and Libraries for Kent; Mrs. A. Fynmore; Peter Guilmant for his line drawings; Mrs. E. Levett; Maidstone Museums and Art Gallery; Ms. Brenda Mason, Curator of Bexhill Museum; Mrs. N. Millen; Mr. Mole and other members of staff at Ashford Library; Mr. Brian Packer, Minister of the Unitarian church; Mr. R. W. Pembleton and the Tenterden & District Local History Society; Mr. Brion Purdey, Principal Librarian, Hastings Area; Dr. Ridge; Major W. Michael Robson; Ms. Jane Starling and the staff of Tenterden Library; the Vicar and Churchwardens of the church of St Mildred; Messrs. D. and G. Weaver; J. Weaver; Ms. Victoria Williams, Curator of Hastings Museum; Mr. E. Wilson, Tenterden Town Clerk (retired). Advertisements are reproduced by kind permission of Kent County Council.

To all the above I am most deeply indebted for the loan of their valuable material, their wide knowledge which they have so willingly shared with me and their general help and support at all times. I must also thank my photographer, Mr. Peter Greenhalf, who has spent much time and effort on my behalf.

Introduction

Although the earliest known settlement at Tenterden was Saxon, a Roman road, probably used for transporting iron to Thanet, ran along the ridge close to the present-day St Michael's church. Part of it is still in use today.

The recorded history of Tenterden began in the seventh century, when the area was acquired by the manor of the newly-founded Minster Abbey in Thanet. According to Judith Glover in *The Place Names of Kent*, the name 'Tenterden' comes from the Old English *Tenet Waraden*, denoting the pig pasture of the men of Thanet. It would originally have been a clearing in the forest where pigs were reared. In the autumn they would have been slaughtered and salted in preparation for the winter. We know very little about the early settlement, but it is possible that by the eighth century there was a church dedicated to St Mildred, a much loved abbess and granddaughter of Egbert, founder of Minster Abbey. The parish church still bears her name. Variations of the spelling are 'Tentevardene' (1178), 'Tentwardenn' (1240), and 'Tentyrden' (1255). The first reference to 'Tenterden' in its present form appears in 1610.

In 1305 Edward I visited Tenterden in connection with the draining of the nearby Romney Marsh which, as a grazing area for sheep kept mainly for their wool, has played an important part in the town's history. Tenterden, with its river ports of Smallhythe and Reading Street, became the centre of the weaving industry in the 14th century when Kentish broadcloth was in great demand. By 1331 some of the Flemish weavers encouraged by Edward III to come to this country had settled there.

There were periodic signs of dissent and discontent. The town seems to have suffered some damage during the Peasants' Revolt of 1381 and, although we cannot be sure whether any of the inhabitants of Tenterden took part in Jack Cade's rebellion of 1450, many Kentishmen were involved in this fight against Henry VI's corrupt administration, heavy taxation and oppressive labour laws. In 1428 John Wadden, a follower of Wycliffe, was burnt at the stake in Norwich, becoming Tenterden's first martyr. He was followed by William Carden and Agnes Grebil in 1511.

Tenterden joined the Confederation of the Cinque Ports in 1449/50, as a 'limb' of Rye. The five Cinque Ports and the 'two Antient Towns' (Rye and Winchelsea) had undertaken to supply a certain number of manned and equipped ships for the king's service but Rye, due to the devastation wrought by numerous French raids, was unable to meet its quota. Each town was permitted to draw up its own by-laws, known as the Custumal, for local government under the jurisdiction of a bailiff and jurats. The first bailiff of Tenterden was Thomas Petlesden, whose family arms are displayed on the mizzen sail of the Cinque Port ship in the town's coat of arms. The towns were exempt from national taxation and separate from the legal authority of the rest of the country, and every man who contributed to the fitting out of ships for the fleet was entitled to certain privileges. The Cinque Port barons still have the right to attend the sovereign at the coronation, and official communications are addressed to 'the Mayor and Combarons'. Originally the barons carried the canopy over the king and his consort and sat at the monarch's right hand at the banquet in Westminster Hall. At the coronation of James II in 1685, however, they disgraced themselves by arriving at the abbey so drunk that they dropped the canopy.

William Caxton, the 15th-century father of English printing, was born in the Weald of Kent. It was once thought that Tenterden was his birthplace, but this has now been refuted. The legendary association has, however, been to Tenterden's advantage as in 1928 when a copy of Higden's *Polychronicon*, printed by Caxton in 1482, was presented to the town.

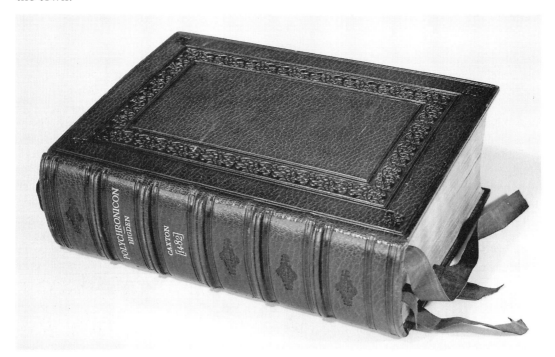

1. This copy of Higden's *Polychronicon* was presented to the town of Tenterden in 1928. The author, Ranulf Higden, was a monk of Chester who died in 1364, and the book is a universal history down to his own times. The book was printed in 1482 by William Caxton, who had set up his printing press in the Almonry at Westminster in 1477.

The 'Town and Hundred of Tenterden' was granted its original charter by Henry VI. The letters patent were issued at Winchester and confirmed by Edward IV at Westminster in 1463. This charter remained valid until the end of Queen Elizabeth's reign.

In 1493 Tenterden was formally linked with Rye under the terms of an elaborate agreement, 'The Composition between Rye and Tenterden', which specified each town's relative position and privileges. It led to many disputes, particularly in connection with the annual payments demanded by Rye, which were to continue until the 18th century. Municipal records dating from 1557-8 refer to the Composition:

> This indenture made the xxi daye of the moneth of September in the eighte yere of the Reigne of Kinge Henrye the seaven after the conquest of Englonde. Between Henry Swane of the Porte and Towne of Rie, Mayor and the Commons of the same Towne of th'one pertye. And Hugh Parker, Bayleye of the Towne and hundred of Tenterden and the Commons of the same Towne and hundred of th'other ptye ...

2. The title page of the Composition made between Rye and Tenterden in 1493.

At this time the Hundred of Tenterden was divided into six boroughs: Town, Boresile, Castweasle, Shrubcote, Reading and Dumborne.

A 16th-century resolution passed at Court Hall concerning the preservation of the town records ran as follows:

> Itt is att this assembly decreed and ordered that all the Records and munimts of the Towne & hundred of Tenterden shalbe p'sently removed and laid in the presse p'vided for that purpose; Except ye Charters and customall which shall remayne in the custody of the Maior for the time being. And except all such Books and Records which the Towne Clerke for the time being shall dailie use or have use of...

The resolution then deals with 'the fowre keyes of the said presse' and how they should be kept. They continued to be mentioned from time to time in the Corporation records but by 1745 there seems to have been only one key.

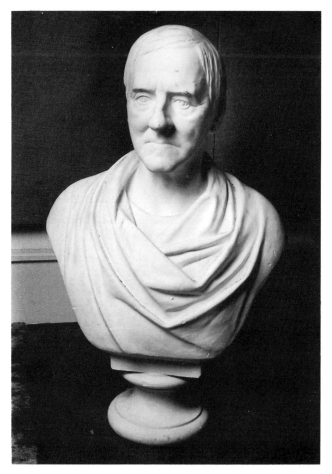

3. Bust of Samuel J. Tilden by an unknown sculptor, dated 1882. In 1634 Nathaniel Tilden, an ancestor of Samuel, emigrated to America and settled in Scituate, Massachusetts. Samuel was nominated for Presidency by the Democrats in 1876 and stood against R. B. Hayes of Ohio, the Republican candidate. The election was disputed and eventually given in favour of Hayes by an *ad hoc* Electoral Commission.

Tenterden's growing importance during the 16th century led to efforts to obtain a new charter and raise the status of the Corporation. A 1539 note found in the Rye Corporation manuscripts states that:

The Mayor of that town, Henry Gaymer, being in London on business, he heard 'news', and accordingly wrote home to the Deputy Mayor William Tolken, that 'Tenterden is taking a new Charter, how far we may be prejudiced therein I pray you think upon and send me your minds'.

Tenterden's new charter was granted in 1600. The style of the Corporation was changed and the bailiff, John Hales, was appointed mayor. Twelve jurats were appointed, nine of whom later served as mayor. The mayor was given custody of the charter at a ceremony held in the Common Hall. After the charter was lost, along with other important records, in a fire in 1661, it was 'exemplified' by William III in 1700.

The charter reflected Tenterden's growing prosperity. Shipbuilding, for example, had become an important industry at Smallhythe where, in 1549, Henry VIII's ship *The Grand Masters* was rebuilt and launched after his death. It weighed 400 tons and could carry 250 armed men. The king visited Tenterden in 1537.

Some inhabitants left England in search of a new life abroad. Nathaniel Tilden, Chamberlain to Tenterden Corporation in 1614/15, emigrated to New England in 1635

4. The Tildens were important clothiers from the 15th to the 18th century. The cloth trade reached its zenith in the 16th century when lighter weaves of cloth were required. Samuel Tilden inherited the family business and three pieces of land at West Cross known as Workhouse field , Barn field and Tenter field. It may be that the name Tenterden derived from the word 'tenter', the frame on which cloth was stretched. John Tilden, Samuel's brother, was Bailiff to Sir Edward Hales. Westwell Farm was built on the site of the old Tilden family home. This photograph was taken *c*.1900.

and settled in Scituate, Massachusetts, where he became town officer and ruling elder. Subsequent emigrations were encouraged by the Poor Law Authority. Sixteen men, three women and one boy, for example, sailed from Rye to the New World on the brig *William* in about 1828, the cost of coach fares and the voyage being met by the authorities.

After the Restoration of Charles II relations between Rye and Tenterden again became strained due to the annual payment of the Composition. In 1655 the matter had been put to the vote and it was unanimously agreed that no payment should be made. In 1661 the mayor of Rye wrote a conciliatory letter to Richard King, mayor of Tenterden, offering to settle for a lesser amount that year in view of the loss of the Court Hall. However the cost of negotiations, entertaining the members for Rye and fees for the Counsel, amounted to £2 17s. – more than the year's Composition – leaving the Corporation out of pocket. In 1762 the mayor and jurats of Rye issued a Bill of Complaint in the High Court of Chancery for the recovery of £4 composition money. The deputy mayor was subpoenaed and the matter had still not been settled two years later.

Many of the documents preserved from this period are very detailed. For several years Robert Gibbon harassed the Corporation for the apparent negligence of Matthew Greenland, the sergeant at mace, in allowing a prisoner, Edward Caister, to escape from jail. The matter was settled many years later when Matthew's son, Joseph, paid £30 in settlement to the Corporation. We can also read of Reginald Mantell who refused to serve as a J.P. in 1710 and was fined £40. It is even recorded that on one occasion the Corporation made a profit of two pence when they impounded a stray colt which they sold the following year. The Corporation was granted an allowance for 'whipping rogues and excuting felons', for which purpose new gallows were erected on the site of the old in 1706. The last execution took place on 27 August 1785.

In 1661 it was decided to build a separate Court Hall and gaol. Timber from the market cross was to be used in the gaol. Later renamed the Town Hall, the building was constructed in 1790 at a cost of £1,000. For some time the Assembly Room was used as the Magistrates' Court; previously Sessions of the Peace had been held at various inns, including the *Woolpack*, the *George* and the *White Lion*. The Mayor's Parlour (originally the card room of the adjoining *Woolpack*) contains portraits of the Curteis family, many of whom served as mayor during the 17th and 18th centuries. It is believed that a serious fire in the 19th century gutted an upper storey, sometimes used as an extension to the inn, which has never been rebuilt. The balcony was added during the present century.

Tenterden seems to have escaped the plague which devastated the population of Rye in the 16th and 17th centuries. In 1665 it became necessary to obtain consent from the authorities before leaving the immediate vicinity of the town. Two Tenterden residents who were deemed 'clean' were allowed to travel to the Isle of Wight.

The parish church of St Mildred dates from the 12th century, though many later additions were made. The parish registers commenced in 1544. Originally written on parchment, they were transcribed into book form in 1599. In the 18th century Dr. Jeremiah Cliff kept a medical record, registering births and deaths. His records, however, do not always agree with those in the parish register, which is believed to be the more accurate of the two. The Anabaptists came to Tenterden in 1704, followed by the Baptists in 1726, the Quakers in 1728 and the Presbyterians in 1761. An early place of worship was The Old Meeting House on the Ashford Road, now the Unitarian church, where Dr. Benjamin Franklin worshipped in 1783. St Michaels Church, built in 1863, is situated to the north of the town. In the outlying hamlets, a small chapel in Smallhythe was mentioned in 1400 when the jurats of Romney paid 3s. 4d. towards its upkeep when a barge was launched. This church was rebuilt in 1516/17, an earlier building having burned down along with most of the hamlet in the early years of the 16th century. Reading Street, on the road to Appledore, is served by the little church of St Mary Ebony, which until 1858 was situated on the remote Isle of Ebony.

From the 13th century onwards a Friday market was held on the High Street greens, and herds of cattle and flocks of sheep were common sights in the town. Until the 18th century the market place was an important focal point in the area. The market cross, repaired by the local blacksmith in 1710, had been used during the Commonwealth years as a place where civil marriages were published. Rogues and vagabonds were chastised at the market house, including William Smith, who pleaded guilty to a charge of petty larceny before Jeremiah Curteis, the mayor, in 1778. He was fined and whipped until his back bled.

During the 18th century Hasted observed that '... there is a small antient market place built of timber, but the market which is still held on a Friday is but little frequented, only two millers & seldom any butchers attending it'. Writing in 1807, less than a century later, Brayley described the Market House as 'a small mean edifice of timber now little frequented, the market itself almost disused'. By 1822 both the house, 'an old wooden fabric tottering under the weight of years', and the market were entirely disused.

The origins of the Tenterden May Fair are unknown. The first surviving reference to it dates from about 1550, when it was recorded that Joan Alcock, widow of Richard Alcock, bailiff, bought her kettle at the 'Fayre of Tenterden'. It was held on the first Monday in May and the first Friday in September. After the First World War, it was moved to the Glebe Fields. In 1977 the May Fair closed.

In the 1830s the population of Tenterden was less than 2,000, and included few professional people. William Cobbett, in *Rural Rides*, described it as a 'small market town and singularly bright spot'. The inhabitants followed a diversity of occupations. They included maltsters, two straw hat manufacturers, a currier, male and female school-teachers, a tallow chandler and a hop merchant – hop-growing was widespread in the area. Many gentlemen were engaged in the grazing business. Cloth-making, once central to Tenterden's economy, was no longer significant although it was still practised to some extent in the 18th century. Breeche's Pond is a reminder of the days when water power was used to make cloth. The tenters, frames on which the cloth was stretched to dry, occupied a south-west facing slope. There were dyemills in the town until the mid-19th century.

The Grammar School, founded in the 14th century, closed *c.*1812 owing to the diminishing number of pupils. It had stood on the same site for nearly 300 years. A National School opened in Church Road in the 1840s.

The London and County Bank opened its Tenterden branch in 1845, subsequently becoming the National Westminster Bank. The Italianate building looks somewhat incongruous amidst the surrounding properties.

Names such as 'Old Barrack Farm' are a reminder of the Napoleonic era, when a garrison was stationed at Reading Street. The racecourse was then at nearby Reading Sewer and was well patronised by the officers. In this area the word 'sewer' retains its medieval meaning of a watercourse for draining marshland. A military road from Ashford to Tenterden was constructed between the years 1798 and 1802 at a cost of £3,300. Many different regiments were engaged on this work, including the 1st West Yorkshires.

Carriers plied the surrounding area and Hollands Waggon ran from the *Eight Bells* to London every Thursday. Coaches also ran regularly to the capital. The 'Tally Ho'

5. A letter, dated Bexhill 17 August 1814, relating to troop movements during the Napoleonic War. The letter reads:

Hon Sir,
   The Route has just Arrived for the German Leigon [sic] to March to Morrow Morning by five O'Clock. The Sargeant which came for the Warrants, Can speak But Little English, and was fearful of stating to you How far the Waggons would be compelld to go, Each stage. The different farmers of this Place will refuse to go to Tenterden being 25 miles unless it is your Order a Warrent for 3 Waggons to Morrow Morning and a Warrent for 6 on Friday Morning.
   I am Hon Sir Your very humble servant
                          Thi Wedd.

A Thomas Wedd lived in Bexhill at this time and it is believed that this letter was written by him.

travelled daily, except on Sundays, from the *Woolpack* to London via Headcorn and Maidstone. The 'Flower of Kent' travelled to London three times a week via Cranbrook and Tonbridge. Letters came by branch post from Lamberhurst.

In December 1899 *The Pictorial Record* described Tenterden as 'one of the most interesting towns in Kent. It is situated in a district teeming with antiquities and memorials of a bygone England, and being ten miles distant from a railway station it retains many features that must have been common to all towns in the old coaching days', and had a reputation for being 'cheerful and lively for its size'. This was certainly true as many societies and clubs flourished, some of which emanated from the church, which would play a far more significant rôle in people's lives than it does today. Local inhabitants were active in producing much of their own entertainment, whether this was of a musical nature or in the form of concert parties. Local dignitaries were generous in loaning the grounds of their houses for many outdoor pursuits, and garden parties were regularly held at Homewood House and Hales Place. The well-known actress, Dame Ellen Terry, lived in the neighbourhood for over 29 years. Today the barn beside her former home, Smallhythe Place, is used for theatre productions. As early as 1912 Tenterden had a cinema which was originally known as the 'Electric Palace'.

Outdoor sports found enthusiastic players and supporters. The town's Goal Running Team is described in caption 142. The Football Club was founded in the 1890s while cricket was played in the town as early as 1755. From 1880 Tenterden held a cricket week which proved popular for many years. There were also a Quoit Club, Bowls Club and Golf Club.

The High Street was the principal business thoroughfare where private houses, business premises, hotels and workshops mingled together. It is generally commercial establishments that take the lead in modernising and improving a town, and Tenterden was no exception to this rule. Many of the leading stores expanded in the early years of this century with fashionable façades. Some of these early shops remained in the same family for generations. The local tradesmen prided themselves on providing their customers with an up-to-date service.

The opening of the small branch line from Robertsbridge, in Sussex, by the Rother Valley Railway had a considerable effect on the town. The name was subsequently changed early in this century to the Kent and East Sussex railway. Authorised in 1896, the line opened in stages between 1900 and 1905. It was one of a group of lines owned by Colonel Stephens and remained a private venture until 1948. The first station serving Tenterden was at Rolvenden; later a more central one opened, becoming known as Tenterden Town station. For many years the line was used for hop-pickers' trains during the season. The line was axed by Beeching in the 1960s, but due to the enthusiasm of a small group of people it has now reopened as far as Northiam and, during the summer months, trains run by a dedicated band of volunteers are a tourist attraction.

From the beginning of the 20th century the town was finding favour with visitors; early guide-books suggested the many beautiful walks which could be taken, together with visits to nearby places of interest.

Tenterden had its own brewery employing local labour. In 1872 it was acquired by Messrs. Edwards and Son who expanded the business. By 1898 a mineral water plant was laid down and the following year was reputed to be 'in full swing'. The brewery was demolished in 1925.

Private schools flourished in this area, particularly in the period between the wars; many were quite small establishments with few pupils, some of whom were boarders.

Visiting parents would have patronised the various inns and hotels in the neighbourhood. The fact that the town was sited in a particularly healthy locality, had a good water supply and from quite early times (*c*.1898) was lighted by gas, may have been an added incentive. St Michael's parish was said to have been one of the first 'villages' in England to adopt acetylene gas.

The Education Committee of Kent County Council purchased Homewood House in 1947 and within two years opened a school there. It is centred round the 1766 mansion which has been described as a 'handsome five storey house with the typical Tenterden cornice'. It possesses a modern hall and since 1968 has had its own swimming pool. Pupils attend from a wide catchment area and the school has an excellent reputation.

The youth of the town are well catered-for, and over the years have had the advantage of their own clubs and organisations. As early as 1973 the Tenterden Youth Club had a modern building in Highbury Lane, providing a variety of indoor activities.

Until 1974, Tenterden was a municipal borough, governed by a borough council presided over by the mayor, and consisting of 12 councillors and four aldermen. However, in that year the town 'lost' its borough status and became a 'successor parish'. In the words of the County Structure Plan: 'The small rural town of Tenterden functions as a service and employment centre, and its unique character, including its countryside setting, make it an important tourist attraction. Conservation and development restraint are overriding objectives ... '. This maxim remains in force today. Much of the town's economy is based on service trades, light industries and agriculture. The latter has always been important to Tenterden, no less today.

No longer does the town boast a market or a theatre, but much beautiful architecture remains. It is unfortunate that some buildings have been demolished since World War Two, among them the Old Manor House, and the early Tudor cottages which at one time adjoined the *White Lion Inn*. However, the High Street's handsome thoroughfare with its trees and stretches of green that separate the footpath from the roadway remain to delight the eye of resident and tourist alike.

Her Majesty Queen Elizabeth the Queen Mother first visited the town as Duchess of York when in 1935 she opened a service training centre for the unemployed. Subsequent visits were made in 1950 and 1982. The Princess of Wales officially opened Tenterden Leisure Centre and swimming pool in Recreation Ground Road on 17 October 1990.

The population of Tenterden has risen from 4,000 in 1900 to 6,200 about ninety years later. The greatest increase has taken place since the 1960s when in round figures it stood at 5,000.

The present council consists of 16 councillors, but no aldermen. Their policy is still to promote the town as a centre for tourism, and in this they are highly successful. They are also interested in increasing all facilities for the local inhabitants and to this end have encouraged further trade in the town with the recent Sayers Lane shopping precinct. Recreation is not overlooked with public tennis courts behind the leisure complex.

From its Saxon beginnings, Tenterden has grown into a prosperous small town, which can now look forward with confidence to the last years of this century, and beyond.

Much of the information in this *Introduction* has been taken from *The Municipal Records of Tenterden*, transcribed by the late A. H. Taylor, and from his articles in *Archaeologia Cantiana*, Volumes 32 and 33. The quotations are taken from these sources unless otherwise stated.

LOCAL GOVERNMENT

6. The earliest reproduction of the Tenterden arms on parchment.

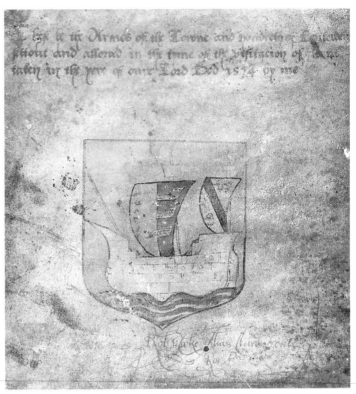

7. The arms of Tenterden, one of the finest of the Cinque Ports, show a three-masted ship with the Ports arms carried on the square sail. The mizzen sail bears the arms of Thomas Petlesden, the town's first Bailiff. Also discernible is the cabin at the stern, the rudder and the anchor.

8. The Great Charter of the Cinque Ports granted during the reign of Edward IV in 1461. The elaborate 'E' takes up nearly half the page.

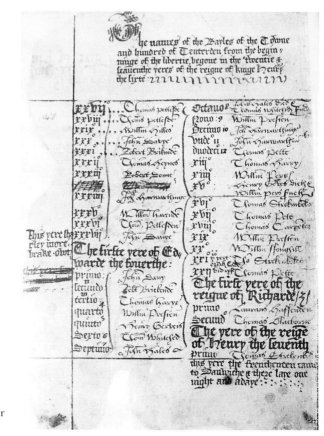

9. The names of the bailiffs (here spelt 'bayles') of the Town and Hundred of Tenterden. When the New Charter was granted in 1600 the bailiff was renamed mayor.

10. (*left*) The first mayoral seal of 1600 showing on the obverse side a single-masted ship bearing the Cinque Ports' arms. The reverse side shows the figure of St Mildred, long associated with the town. This photograph shows the image in reverse because it is taken from the base of the official seal used by the Tenterden Town Council.

11. (*right*) The second mayoral seal of the 17th century was in silver and showed a three-masted ship under full sail.

12. This painting of Robert Curteis, Mayor of Tenterden in 1632, hangs in the Mayor's Parlour.

TO THE INHABITANTS OF
TENTERDEN
PEACE AND CONCORD. SEND GREETING!
TREASON! HIGH TREASON!!

TENTERDEN, (TO WIT)

WE the Top Sawyers of Tenterden, charge and command all our loving Subjects to Curfew all their Fires, and immediately upon Sight hereof, to close, shut up, fasten and barricade all their respective Houses and Dwellings, Shops and Out-houses within our Dominions; and that they will likewise shut up and incarcerate themselves, their Wives, Children, and Servants within the premises aforesaid, henceforth until the coming Election shall be over, past, gone, finished and closed.

FOR BE IT KNOWN unto all Christian people, that a High Peace Officer has diligently and by Virtue of his High Office discovered A PLOT!

A HORRIBLE CONSPIRACY!!!

not to Guy Faux, our Liege Subjects into Eternity with
THREE SCORE BARRELS LAID BELOW!!!

but that the Authority aforesaid, hath actually discovered and made known unto our trusty and well beloved first Law Officer of the Crown, that a plot has been devised and planned by a certain evil disposed person called, "HOOKY," instigated by the Devil with divers others of the same Kidney, evil disposed and instigated in like manner as aforesaid, and that such persons have put and placed, laid up and secreted

150 ROTTON AND ADDLED EGGS!!

against the day of Election at Tenterden, on the 3rd. day of August Instant, IN ORDER then, and there, and thereby, and therewith, Evilly and with Malice aforethought to tarnish, sully, soil, bespangle, bespatter, besmear, begrime, damage, hurt, injure, prejudice and damnify the Sunday Clothes of all our loving Subjects, then and there to be exhibited, put on, worn and displayed, and against the peace of our printed List of Town Councillors.

Given at our Court at Tenterden this 1st. day of August in the 2nd. year of our Reign.

GOD SAVE THE QUEEN!!

13. This poster probably refers to the Chartist Movement. The Chartists' demands were for universal manhood suffrage, secret ballots and equal electoral districts. The disenfranchised of Tenterden seem to be threatening to disrupt the Town Council elections with '150 rotten and addled eggs'. Records of the Tenterden Mutual Improvement Society show that there were Chartist sympathisers in Tenterden in 1848, when the movement came to an abrupt end following the cancellation of a procession to present a monster petition to Parliament.

14. The Tenterden maces. The largest is of silver gilt, dated 1549 and 1660. The first date refers to the 100th anniversary of the granting of the charter, while the second refers to the Restoration of King Charles II. The silver mace is also dated 1660. The pocket mace has the Royal Arms at one end and the Cinque Port ships engraved at the other. It weighs 15ozs. An account dated 1652 states that two new maces had been acquired with the Arms of the State, one a very small pocket mace. The cost totalled £7 7s. 6d.

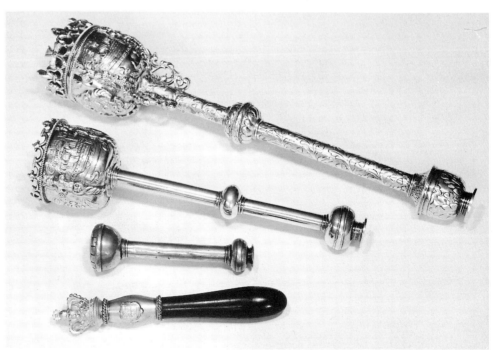

15. Stephen Goodsall and Nelson Tickner, mace bearers. The former was appointed 2nd Sergeant at Mace as early as 1867 and in 1902 he became the 1st Sergeant at Mace. By January 1917 he had completed 50 years service with Tenterden Corporation.

16. Mayor's Day, 1920. Alderman Edgar Howard, Coronation Baron, and Alderman Herbert Nieve, Mayor of Tenterden, are preceded by the mace bearers.

CHURCHES

The parish church of St Mildred dates from the 12th century. The oldest part is the chancel, with an original lancet window in the north wall and a piscina in the south-east corner. The next century saw the addition of the south aisle and a porch, on which are the scratch dials which indicated the time of masses. During the 15th century the church was again enlarged because Tenterden had become an important centre of the cloth industry. Peter Marshall founded a chantry (1494-1512), the endowment coming from various houses and lands in and around Tenterden, including the *Woolpack Inn*. The money thus raised was for the support of a chaplain and for teaching the boys at the Grammar School. In 1655 Oliver Cromwell presented the living to George Hawe but he was deprived of office after the Restoration of the Monarchy. The church suffered years of neglect and it was not until the 19th century that much needed restoration work was undertaken; at that time the galleries and box pews were removed. The present church tower was built in 1461, the lower part constructed of Bethersden marble. As early as 1475, the tower had become part of a beacon warning system against the French and subsequently the Spanish, at the time of the Armada. In times of danger a saddled horse stood in readiness in a rough stable close to the church.

17. St Mildred's Church showing the old clock face, *c*.1880. A new clock was installed on the occasion of Queen Victoria's Jubilee.

8. (*above*) St Mildred's Church, Tenterden. The building on the right of the picture was once a Police Station, built on the site of the wooden tollhouse which was demolished *c*.1880. Subsequently it became Rye Model Laundry, but for many years the bars of the police cells could be seen behind the counter.

9. (*above right*) The unusual double west door of St Mildred's Church. There is only one other such double door in Kent.

10. In 1864 Mr. Benjamin Hatch gave the vicar of St Mildred's this mutilated alabaster carving of the Resurrection which he had found at Leigh Green. It may be part of the missing representation of the Resurrection, broken at the time of the Reformation or during the Commonwealth. Today this carving can be seen above the doorway to the rood stairs in the church.

21.   The interior of St Mildred's Church in 1867.

22.   Interior of the church in 1910.

23. Bishop's stonemason's yard next to the Zion Baptist Chapel in 1870 before the alterations to the façade took place in 1887. This building in the High Street is still a Baptist chapel today. Unfortunately the old house on the right was demolished in 1874.

24. Zion Baptist Chapel, erected in 1835. In 1887 the building was renovated in a style reminiscent of a Greek temple, as can be seen in this print which was produced in about 1890.

25. The Wesleyan Chapel, Tenterden. This drawing appeared in Thomson's *Local Directory and Almanac* in 1889, along with the following description: 'The new Wesleyan Chapel, situate at West Cross, is a beautiful Fifteenth Century Gothic structure, with Cathedral tinted glass windows. It was opened in April, 1885, by the Rev. F. Greeves, D.D., President of the Conference. At the rear of the Chapel are commodious School and Classrooms. The entire cost was about £2,300.' In 1889 the minister was the Rev. T. Rising.

26. The Old Meeting House, Ashford Road, today known as the Unitarian Church. Early dissenting congregations were not permitted to build their own places of worship until the passing of the Act of Toleration in 1689 and it is believed that the first Meeting House was erected about this time. It was rebuilt at about the time of the Rev. Cornelius Handcock's arrival in the locality and was registered in September 1746 as a place of worship used by 'the protestant Presbyterian dissenters living in or near Tenterden'. On the outside wall of the building is a plaque to Benjamin Franklin, the American scientist and statesman who visited the Meeting House when his friend Dr. Joseph Priestley preached there in 1783. In front of the Meeting House is the tombstone of the Rev. Lawrence Holden who served as minister for 72 years.

27. The interior of the Meeting House, showing the fine pulpit with sounding board and one of the galleries.

STREET SCENES

8.   Tenterden tollgate from an 18th-century engraving. The gate stood in the narrow part of the High Street and was removed in 1880; it was apparently burnt at the annual Guy Fawkes' Day bonfire 'amid great rejoicings' from the population. There were over 50 turnpike trusts in Kent which had improved roads but also levied tolls on vehicles using them.

29. The tollgate and tollhouse *c*.1875, looking eastward along the High Street. The building on the right-hand side is known as The Pebbles and is now Tenterden Library. The wooden tollhouse was at one time used as the town's lock-up.

30. In 1880 the building in the centre of this photograph was erected on the site of the old tollhouse and for many years it served as the Police Station. On the left is James Puxted's cycle shop, and next to that is the Temperance Hotel, within the same building.

31. This 18th-century milestone, erected by the local turnpike trust, was removed during World War Two but has since been restored to its original position between the old tollgate and the line of posts in front of The Pebbles (see plate 29).

32. A sketch of Tenterden in 1860, by A. Phipson. The splendid pinnacled tower of the church was ever a reminder to the inhabitants of the town's former importance as a centre of the weaving industry.

33. A bird's-eye view of the western portion of the High Street in about 1910, photographed from the church tower.

34. An etching of the High Street by E. McLaughlin, dated 1938.

35. This picture, taken early in the century, shows one of the town pumps. The important stock fairs were originally held in this wide stretch of the High Street lying between the former tollgate and West Cross.

36. A similar view taken in about 1930 when the pump had been removed.

TENTERDEN. HIGH STREET.

37. Tenterden High Street looking east, c.1905. On the right is the *Black Horse Inn*, now renamed the *William Caxton*. At one time Tenterden claimed to be the birthplace of Caxton but there is no evidence to support this theory, although the Caxtons were known to have lived in Kent. Opposite the inn is Milsted's Forge and Ironworks; many railings and gates made by Milsted's can be seen in and around Tenterden today.

38. This advertisement appeared in Thomson's *Directory* in 1889.

39.   The narrow part of the High Street sometime after 1910, when this type of telegraph pole was erected in the town. The timber-framed building on the left was for many years the home of the Hook family, butchers in the High Street. Today the original shop is occupied by 'Book Shelves' and the family's living quarters are occupied by the Tudor Rose restaurant. A restaurant of this name has been there since the 1920s.

40.   Tenterden has long been regarded as the capital of the Weald, and many of its buildings are very imposing. The tall one, adjoining the timbered structure, was a corn chandler's residence and warehouse; like others in the town it is timber-framed with mathematical tiles simulating bricks, set with wood quoins at the angles.

41. & 42.   Two views of Tenterden in the snow, *c*.1920.

43. Golden Cross, *c*.1905. The small building on the right was at one time the *Plough* beerhouse, which would have sold ale brewed locally.

44. East Cross, *c*.1930. Behind the trees and signpost was the Picture Theatre built in 1912; today this building has been developed as shops and offices and is known as The Fairings (see plate 140).

45. Ashford Road, *c*.1900. On the left-hand side are the premises of a long established firm; at this time Mr. Thomas Avery practised as a plumber and decorator.

46. An unusual view of Bells Lane looking north into the High Street. The *Eight Bells* public house is a fine example of a cantilevered upper storey or jetty.

47.   Bells Lane, *c.*1910. Tenterden theatre was built here in the 18th century and many of the cottages today
have names relating to this, for example Theatre Cottage and Playwright Cottage. Nearby is a small brick
building with a sign denoting 'Soup Kitchen' above the door, and the date 1875. Perhaps relief in the form
of soup was needed during the agricultural depression of the 1870s and '80s.

APPS & SON,

Builders' and

FURNISHING IRONMONGERS,

LAMP AND OIL MERCHANTS,

EAST CROSS, TENTERDEN.

IMPLEMENT
AND
MACHINE
AGENTS,
&C.

PORTABLE KITCHENERS, STOVES & RANGES,

Mangling and Wringing Machines,

Galvanized Roofing, Wire Netting, Carpenters' and other Tools,

POWDER, SHOT AND CARTRIDGES,

TABLE & POCKET CUTLERY. ELECTRO-PLATED GOODS,

LAMPS OF EVERY DESCRIPTION, BEST CRYSTAL OILS,

New work in Tin, Copper and Zinc, made to order at Moderate Prices.

Repairs of all kinds Promptly and Neatly Executed.

Oil Van calls regularly throughout the Neighbourhood,

all orders executed with despatch,

Sole Agent for the ROVER, CENTAUR & STAR CYCLES
Other makes procured.

48. This advertisement appeared in Thomson's *Directory* in 1900.

49. Mr. E. P. Apps traded as 'Ironmonger, Brazier, Tinman, etc.' as advertised on his shop fascia in this photograph, *c*.1860. Mr. Apps may be the gentleman standing in the doorway, wearing a leather apron. The shop was demolished in 1865 in order to make way for a branch of the London & County Bank.

50. Mr. Apps transferred his business to other premises in the High Street and, as can be seen, his business flourished.

51. Field's hairdresser's shop, *c.*1910. This shop can also be seen in plate 50.

52. Mr. E. Stanger took over an existing grocery business in 1871 and within a decade he had constructed this new frontage and refurbished and modernised the shop and warehouse. This photograph was taken in 1899.

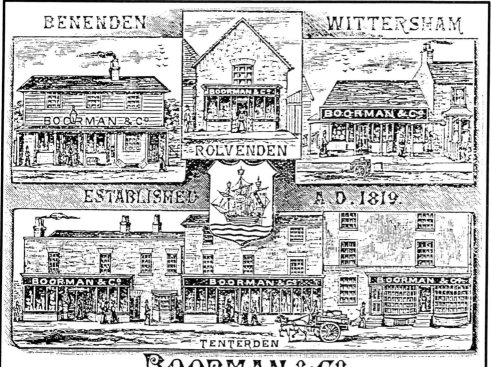

BENENDEN   WITTERSHAM

BOORMAN & C?

ROLVENDEN

ESTABLISHED   A.D. 1819.

TENTERDEN

BOORMAN & C?
GROCERS, DRAPERS, OUTFITTERS, BOOT MERCHANTS,
& COMPLETE HOUSE FURNISHERS,
WEST CROSS, TENTERDEN.

53a. & b. These two advertisements appeared in Thomson's *Directory* around the turn of the century. Samuel Boorman founded the business in 1819 and the premises comprised three houses, the frontage extending over 100 ft. The shop sold groceries and provisions, clothing for both men and women, boots and shoes, and home furnishings. Boorman's warehouses and offices were at the rear of the shop, approached by a side roadway. Boorman & Co. closed after 150 years of trading, most of the buildings were demolished and the site redeveloped.

54. Shops in the High Street, *c*.1890. The meat is hanging outside Hook's butcher's shop. Above the furnishing shop on the right is a pulley used to load hay into the store above.

55. Ellen Mercer in front of the family shop in Station Road, *c*.1910. This business moved to the High Street in 1914.

56. By 1914 the Mercer family business had expanded so much that it could no longer operate from their home in Station Road. This undated photograph shows a monster 17lb. cabbage on a barrow outside Mercer's shop in the High Street. On the left is John Mercer and on the right Charles Mercer. Like many other shopkeepers they had their own hand-barrow for home deliveries.

57. A 1914 line drawing of the *White Lion* by D. C. Maynard. The adjacent cottages have subsequently been demolished.

58. The timber-framed building on the left was erected in about 1780 by Dr. John Mace. Known today as The Pebbles, it has a high central doorway through which Dr. Mace could ride direct to the stable at the rear. The building is hung with mathematical tiles, as is the *White Lion* next door. On the right-hand side of this turn-of-the-century photograph can be seen the carriage arch of the 16th-century inn.

59. R. Weeks & Sons claimed to be the biggest and best known firm of builders in and around Tenterden in 1899. Their premises, sited next to the *White Lion Hotel*, consisted of offices, workshops, stores, a yard and stabling for six horses. They stocked all kinds of timber, sanitary goods, drain-pipes, bricks and other building tools and materials. Messrs. Weeks & Sons were also funeral furnishers and claimed to carry out interments in any part of the country.

60. Charabanc outside Lewis and Hyland, drapers and house furnishers, *c.*1925. Unfortunately it has been impossible to confirm whether this was an outing to the coast organised for the employees of the firm, which served Tenterden for many years until it closed in 1986.

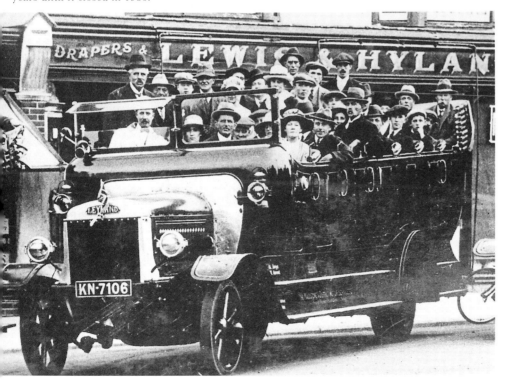

61. The International Stores was one of the first of the multiple stores to arrive in Tenterden in the early years of the 20th century. The company always photographed their staff, dressed correctly in their white aprons and standing in front of the shop. This photograph was taken in about 1910.

62.   This 15th-century black and white house was originally a 'hall-house', being altered in the following century both internally and by the addition of the chimney stack at the east end. Formerly smoke from a central fire would have been allowed to escape through the roof. At the time this photograph was taken, c.1890, the shop and house were occupied by Stephen Hook; behind the house were open fields and also a slaughter-house. Mr. Hook carried on the business for nearly 50 years.

63.   Meat on display at Hook's at Christmastide 1902.

PROMINENT BUILDINGS

64.   The *Woolpack Inn* and the Town Hall prior to the erection of the balcony in 1912.

Town Hall, Tenterden.

65. The Town Hall, adjoining the *Woolpack Inn*, was built in 1790, to replace the original hall which burnt down in 1661. The graceful ironwork balcony was added in 1912, but access could only be achieved by replacing the original Venetian window with the one shown in this picture. Within the building is an Assembly Room which was once the Magistrates' Court. The ivy-clad building behind the tree is part of the inn. This photograph was taken *c.*1920.

66. The musicians gallery in the Assembly Room of the Town Hall has recently been restored to its original beauty.

67. Ivy Court has had a chequered history. Built in the 18th century, it was formerly the home of the Avery family who were at one time connected with the nearby *Olde Cellars* public house. The large tract of land to the west of the house was sold and a cinema erected there in 1938. This overshadowed the house and added little to the charm of Tenterden. Shops were built in the front of Ivy Court garden, although the house could still be reached through its own front door, brought forward at the end of a corridor and on the same building line as the shop fronts.

68. Front elevation of Ivy Court, showing the two shop fronts standing between the original ornate doorway which had been brought forward to the new building line. The large building to the west was originally the Embassy Cinema and is now a supermarket.

69. Interior of *Ye Olde Cellars* public house, now called *The Cellars*, showing the cards, photographs and letters which decorated the ceiling. These naturally became quite a topic of conversation with residents and visitors alike and many people began to mail them from all parts of the world.

70. Today The Armoury is divided into cottages behind a unified Georgian façade. In the 19th century it was the headquarters of the Tenterden detachment of the Cinque Ports Rifle Volunteers, formed in 1859 to fight Napoleon III.

71.   Finchden Manor, sometimes known as The Priory, has seen many changes throughout the years. The Tudor-style building was leased to the Benedictine order of monks from 1875; they occupied it for over 30 years. During the last war the building was requisitioned by the Army and at the end of hostilities it became a home for young emotionally disturbed boys, which operated until 1974. The name Finchden is associated with the Finch family, prominent in Tenterden in the medieval period. When Mr. Lyward, the owner, died in the 1970s the house was sold to pay death duties.

72.   This pseudo-Tudor house called The Grange was at one time the home of the Diggle family and the gentleman sitting beside the croquet lawn may be Joseph McCrae Diggle who was mayor of Tenterden on a number of occasions. The building was at one time used as a school. During World War Two it was badly damaged by a bomb and subsequently demolished, being replaced by a much smaller house on the site.

73. Hales Place. Although much of the original house was demolished in the middle of the 18th century, what remains is very impressive. There is an Elizabethan garden with two two-storeyed pavilions at the east corners. Note the impressive entrance arch to the right of the main building.

74. Seventeenth-century grotesque brackets on the front door of Hales Place.

75. The Gothic-style mansion of Heronden Hall. The name 'Heronden' is of great antiquity and the manor was the subject of a charter in 968. The drawing, by X. Willis, first appeared in *A Saunter Through Kent with Pen and Pencil* by Charles Igglesden, published in 1902.

76. The interior of Heronden Hall. The architect was A. J. Donthorne, who designed the house for William Curteis Whelan in 1853. Heronden Hall replaced Heronden Parva, a medieval timber-framed house which stood not far from the present gatehouse.

77. Gatehouse to Heronden Hall, built in the Gothic style. This building was badly damaged in the hurricane of 1987, and today the small extension on the right-hand side is partially demolished.

78. The *Black Horse Inn* c.1934, looking towards the Gatehouse of Heronden Hall.

79. A cycling club assembled by Heronden Gateway, *c*.1900. Cycling was extremely popular with members of both sexes and they often travelled long distances on club outings, the roads being far less congested than they are today.

EDUCATION

80. The Old Grammar School from an engraving by H. Buckley, dated 1824. Originally built as a hall house, it became a school in the 16th century, closing in 1812. Today the building is a shop, though somewhat altered in appearance.

81. The Old Grammar School, c.1900. A free grammar school must already have been in existence by 1521 because in that year a gift was made to it. In such a 'free' grammar school, only instruction in Latin and Greek was free; if the scholars wanted to be taught other subjects such as English, writing or arithmetic, they had to pay a fee to the master.

HIGH SCHOOL FOR GIRLS,

The Limes, Tenterden, Kent.

Principal—MISS SOMMERS.

Thorough Education and Careful Home Training.

The course of study comprises the usual English subjects; French, German, Vocal and Instrumental Music, Theory and Harmony; Drawing in all Styles. Painting in Oils and Water Colors; Calisthenics and Dancing.

Pupils prepared for Oxford, Cambridge, College of Preceptors, The Kensington Local (English and Music), Royal Academy of Music, International College of Music Examinations.

All subjects taught by trained and certificated Teachers.

During the last year candidates have been presented in the following :
THE KENSINGTON LOCAL, 17 passed in English subjects, &c.; in Practical Music 13 sat and *all* passed, 2 obtaining honors. At the INTERNATIONAL COLLEGE OF MUSIC, 6 were successful and 1 also at the ROYAL ACADEMY OF MUSIC, making a total of 37 PUBLIC CERTIFICATES obtained since April, 1888.

Prospectus and References on application to Principal. N.B.—*Vacancies for Boarders.*

---

82. Advertisement from Thomson's *Local Directory and Almanac*, 1889. Tenterden was for many years a popular town for small private schools. The same *Directory* advertises 'Beacon Oak Boarding and Day School, Tenterden' in 1900 and 'Gatesdene School, A Home Boarding School for Girls' in 1926. The latter made provision for 'Daily Boarding for Pupils coming from Rolveden, Benenden, High Halden, Woodchurch and all surrounding villages'.

83. During the early years of the century this was Penderel School; today the building is known as Penderel Court. The section nearest the Old Meeting House is Chapel House, home of the Minister.

84. The old schoolhouse in Ashford Road. From 1820 the Dissenters had their own Sunday School, established to provide a basic but free education for children of poor families. A school room was added to the rear of the Meeting House in 1838. Subsequently this purpose-built school was erected, known as the British School. Today the building is a private house but it retains many of its original features.

35. Pupils from the National School, a Church of England foundation, *c*.1900. Children from the Union Workhouse attended this school, usually identifiable by their cropped hair and by their uniform of brown dresses and hats, covered by black cloaks. The young person third from left in the back row may have been a pupil-teacher, as she looks very little older than her charges.

MILLS

86. Ashbourne Mill. Tenterden was unusual in having a watermill and a windmill adjacent to one another. This picture shows the latter in a semi-derelict state. The windmill was a well-built structure of the open-tripod type, erected in 1807 by the millwright, Ralph of Sissinghurst, for Mr. Boorman of Tenterden. One pair of sweeps was removed c.1908 and for a time the mill was run with only two; it finally ceased operating in about 1910. For a time it was known as Pinyon's mill after one of the millers. The watermill was to the left of the buildings behind the tree.

87. Ashbourne watermill, c.1910: an 18th-century three-storey brick and timber building.

88. At one time there were seven windmills in the Tenterden area. This photograph shows the demolition of Pinyon's Mill in 1912. The structure had become unsafe, particularly during high winds. The mill was pulled over by a wire rope attached to a traction engine.

89. This smock mill at Leigh Green, erected in 1818, was the last of the mills in and around Tenterden to operate. It was destroyed by fire in 1913. An early miller, Stephen Judge, once walked from Tenterden to the Corn Market at Canterbury and back in a day. This was during the Crimean War and he rightly judged that corn would increase in price and so was anxious to buy before it was beyond his means. The mill came to be known as Pilbeams after Mr. J. Pilbeam who bought it in 1887. The mill is shown here in about 1905.

90a. & b. Pilbeams Mill was destroyed by a fire which swept through the building on 26 November 1913. Little of the original structure survived and none above the external circular walkway. It is said that the mill was working at 10 p.m. and well alight an hour later.

PUBLIC SERVICES

91. Before the provision of a main water supply many houses were dependent on wells, sometimes reinforced by water mills such as the one shown in this picture, *c*.1910.

92. Construction of Tenterden town sewers in Pittlesden Farm field, 1913.

93.   Tenterden Borough police force in 1889, prior to their amalgamation with Kent County Council.

94.   Tenterden's fire brigade goes into action, *c.*1900.

95.   Tenterden fire brigade outside the old station, *c.*1905. This building has now been demolished. The horses were stabled at the rear so that they were easily accessible when needed.

AGRICULTURE IN & AROUND TENTERDEN

96. Tenterden from Six Fields, *c*.1935, showing the rural setting of the town.

97. A Kentish turn-wrest plough.

98. The May Fair, *c.*1890. Sheep and cattle were driven into the town from the surrounding countryside and many local children took time off from school to help. The old house on the left is the Pittlesden Gatehouse, reputed to be one of the oldest houses in Tenterden. The sheep are believed to be Kent and Romney Marsh flocks. Tradesmen complained of the smell from the fairs, so they were later held on the Glebe Field.

99. Eighteenth-century buildings on the north side of the High Street, originally a turnpike road constructed in 1762. All the buildings are timber-framed and many are either of weatherboarding or painted stucco. The trees were planted in 1871 and for many years the sheep fairs and cattle markets were held on the wide green verges on the south side of the road. The photograph was taken in about 1910, but the scene is little different today apart from the numerous parked cars.

100. Sheep washing in the river Rother, *c.*1905.

101. From earliest times the land around Tenterden has been used for swine grazing, sheep pasture, arable and meadow. Sheep in particular have always been associated with Romney Marsh. In the medieval period cargoes of wool were exported from Smallhythe, the river port serving Tenterden. This photograph shows shearing taking place in the open on the Marsh, *c.*1920.

102. This advertisement appeared in Thomson's *Directory* in 1899.

103a. & b.   Flocks of sheep were a familiar sight in Tenterden High Street and Ashford Road until well into the 1970s; much of the prosperity of the town was founded on wool and cloth. The photograph above was taken in about 1920 and the one below in about 1950.

104.   Threshing on a farm in Kent, *c.*1890.

105.   Haymaking was hot, thirsty work for both men and women. Water was transported in stone jugs or jars to keep it cool. This photograph was taken *c.*1890.

106.   Oxen on a farm near Tenterden, with Ambrose Bull on the waggon, *c*.1870. Before mechanisation many of the farms in the area would have used teams of both oxen and horses.

107.   Mr. Wilfred Clark, a chicken farmer, seen here with his birds, *c*.1930. The farm was situated at the end of Bells Lane. After World War One many ex-servicemen ran small farms such as these but often had difficulty in making a living.

HOP PICKING & BREWING

108. An unknown child hop-picker, *c.*1890. This picture was taken by John Barnes of Tenterden.

109a. & b.   Many farmers grew hops as a cash crop during the 19th century, but the large gardens in Kent operated as commercial enterprises, many of them being owned by the brewery companies. During 1880 Kent produced 42,977 tons of hops, far more than any other county. However, by 1910 this figure had fallen to 28,169 tons. Many of the pickers came from London and at times caused some social problems due to their somewhat 'Bohemian' life-style. These photographs were taken in about 1910.

110. Tallyman with his tally sticks, 1900. These sticks were always in pairs and the tallyman was responsible for cutting notches in both, giving one to the hop-picker and retaining the other himself. The hops were picked into bins and the measurer came round three or four times during the day. The hops were then placed in bushel baskets, and 10 bushels of hops were put into a poke or green bag and loaded onto a waggon. From the gardens the hops were taken to the oast and laid out to keep cool until they were put into the kiln to dry overnight.

111.   Beer drinking was very popular towards the end of the Victorian period and hops became an important part of the economy of Kent. They were expensive to plant but the attendant woodland industries, such as hop-pole shaving, gave a living to many who would otherwise have been unemployed.

112.   An interior picture showing hop pressing in operation.

113. Hop demonstrations took place throughout Kent in 1908. This picture shows the one at Tenterden on 9 May, when the local farmers protested against the importation of foreign hops.

114. Souvenir poster for the Monster Hop Demonstration to be held in Trafalgar Square, London, on 16 May 1908.

115. Mr. G. Crouch taking a poke of hops to the station in about 1920.

116. With so many hops grown in the vicinity of Tenterden, it is not surprising that the town had its own brewery with its own system of transport. This van, photographed *c.*1920, delivered crates of beer to many local establishments.

— TENTERDEN BREWERY. —
WINE AND SPIRIT STORES.

O. EDWARDS & SONS,
(LATE R. C. M. YOUNG.)

GENUINE HOME BREWED FAMILY ALES

		per gallon.
Superior Family Bitter Ales	XXX	1 6
Ditto Mild	XXX	1 6
Ditto Mild	XX	1 4
Ditto Mild Beer	X	1 0
Bitter Beer	X	1 0
Ditto T Beer		10
SS Stout		1 6
— Stout		1 4
London Porter		1 0
Table Beer		8

WINES & SPIRITS OF THE BEST QUALITY

	per gallon.
Jersey Brandy	2 6
Best Cognac Brandy (pale or brown)	4 6
Best Unsweetened Gin	2 6
Finest Old Tom Gin	2 6
Royal Highland Whisky	3 6
Finest Irish Malt Ditto	3 6
Old Jamaica Rum	2 6
Ditto	2 6
Best Cordial Gin	2 0

ALL ORDERS PROMPTLY ATTENDED TO.
All Wines of the best quality at the lowest possible **Prices.**

117. Such advertisements for Tenterden Brewery appeared in Thomson's *Directory* for many years around the turn of the century.

OTHER TRADES & CRAFTS

118. Charcoal was used in the drying of hops. The workers lived in very primitive surroundings, often travelling from farm to farm. The work was extremely hard and the rewards few as the men were separated from their families for long stretches at a time. This photograph was taken *c.*1890.

119. The exterior of the West Cross premises of Messrs. R. & J. Bennett & Co., omnibus proprietors, general carriers and coal and coke merchants, 1899.

120. Bennett's business began early in the 19th century and it remained in the same family for nearly 150 years. Their extensive premises at West Cross consisted of offices, a yard and good stabling, furnished with roomy stalls and boxes. They grew much of their fodder on their farm at London Beach near High Halden and were renowned for providing the best prepared food for their stud of over 40 horses. Bennett & Co. supplied carriages for weddings and other festivities; they also ran omnibuses into the surrounding area and ran a special express service from Tenterden to London, allowing the traveller approximately six hours in the capital before the return journey. The firm also claimed to provide the best and cheapest coal in Tenterden. The yard is now Bennetts Mews.

121. Coach building at Tenterden, *c.*1900. Mr. W. T. Mercer acquired the land in Woodchurch Road and erected these purpose-built premises during the last decade of the 19th century. Adjoining this building, but quite separate from it, was the smith's shop where the 'carriages' or metal underwork were made and put together. The ground floor was occupied by what was technically known as the body-making and wheel shops, and on the upper storey, which was reached by an inclined plane up which the carriages were wheeled by a powerful crabb, housed the trimming and paint shops, great pains being taken to exclude dust and to keep the shop at an even temperature. Mr. Mercer's vehicles, which ranged from smart broughams to tradesmen's vans, were described as 'good work at moderate prices'.

122. This advertisement appeared in the 1890 Thomson's *Directory.*

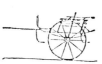 **H. F. GOLDSMITH,**

⤙ Coach Builder. ⤚

Carriages

OF

every description built to order on the most approved principles at moderate charges.

━━┼┼━━

DESIGNS ON APPLICATION.

━━┼┼━━

Carriages

OF

every description Repaired, Painted, & Trimmed neatly and expeditiously.

━━┼┼━━

ESTIMATES FREE,

━━┼┼━━

⤙ **OAK'S HOUSE, TENTERDEN.** ⤚

India Rubber, Brake Blocks, Lamps, Rugs, Mats, and every Requisite supplied to order.

CARRIAGES TAKEN IN EXCHANGE AND WAREHOUSED.

123. Hides arriving at the old Tannery in Smallhythe Road, *c.*1910, having been collected from all parts of the county. For many years the smell from the Tannery permeated the streets of the town.

124. In 1925 Kent County Council borrowed a blacksmith's demonstration van from the Ministry of Agriculture. The van was equipped with an oil-engine lathe, anvil, portable forge, an acetylene welding cutting plant, emery grinder, work-bench and vices. The aim was to help rural smiths to increase their knowledge of modern equipment and thus improve their work. The van avoided the large towns and concentrated on the rural areas, normally spending three to five days at each centre. Many smiths took advantage of this scheme and benefited from individual instruction. Boys from local elementary schools were also invited to attend these demonstrations. The van was in use for under a year but during that time 362 smiths took advantage of its facilities.

G. BARDEN,

𝔊mith, 𝔈ngineer, &c.

AND

CYCLE MANUFACTURER,

TENTERDEN.

Perambulators re-tired.
Lightning Conductors constructed and existing Conductors tested.

𝔅y 𝔅oyal 𝔏etters 𝔓atent.

SEND FOR LIST.

SEND FOR LIST.

The New Patent Safety Lady's Bicycle.

125. This advertisement appeared in the 1890 issue of Thomson's *Directory*.

126. Tenterden High Street early this century, with the Police Station on the left. The horse-drawn vehicle on the right is thought to be Hook's horse bus which plied for trade between Tenterden station and the town.

127. Frank Clarke driving Hook's horse bus, a vehicle which carried a maximum of six passengers, and operated for the Rother Valley Railway. It ran between Tenterden station, the town, and surrounding area. The photograph was taken *c.*1900.

128.   A European air race was organised by the *Standard* newspaper and the Paris *Journal* in July 1911. The *Kentish Express and Ashford News* described the 11 planes taking part as 'like a flight of swallows'. They flew across the Channel by way of Shoreham, and their course was mapped out by a series of large white arrows on the ground. This photograph shows a Renaux in full flight near Reading Street, Tenterden. This particular plane was forced to make an emergency landing due to a fault in the carburettor.

129.   Many local people flocked to view the grounded plane on Romney Marsh.

130.   The winter of 1925-6 was a particularly wet one in the south-east of England and many vehicles were marooned in floods. This picture shows Bennett's bus stuck in deep water on the Wittersham Road near the *Barge Inn*.

131. The railway track looking towards Tenterden from the west, *c.*1910. The tall chimney visible on the right was part of Tenterden Brewery; this stood behind the *Vine Inn* in Station Road. The Brewery was run for many years by Messrs. O. Edwards and Son but closed during the 1920s. The chimney was demolished in 1925.

132. Tenterden station from the church tower in 1934. The station building was erected in 1903.

133. A K. & E.S.R. train at Tenterden Town station in 1934.

134. The railcar which operated on the line between Headcorn and Robertsbridge, *c*.1940. The Kent and East Sussex Railway, which opened in stages between 1900 and 1905, was one of a group of lines owned by Colonel Stephens and remained a private venture until 1948 when it was nationalised. It became a casualty of the Beeching 'axe', closing to traffic in 1961. Today it is a tourist attraction, running a unique collection of rolling stock and locomotives between Tenterden and Northiam. The railway company acquired two railcars, Ford trucks powered by petrol-driven engines, which competed with the local bus company.

LEISURE & PLEASURE

135. & 136. In 1906 Tenterden had a company of the Boys Brigade (*above*). Two years later the Tenterden troop of Boy Scouts was formed, many of the members transferring from the Boys Brigade. In 1911 Tenterden scouts went to a camp in Windsor Great Park (*below*) which was reviewed by the King.

137. Tenterden scouts in 1934. Among those shown are Lt. Col. W. A. V. Finlater, Stanley Head, George Austen and Jack Bazzard.

Tenterden Races.

In consequence of the TONBRIDGE-WELLS RACES, being fixed the 20th Instant, Tenterden RACES, are unavoidably postponed to MONDAY the 25th Instant.

The Horses to be enter'd on Saturday the 23rd; See former advertisement. *Tenterden August 7th 1817*

138. An old poster from Tenterden Museum collection relating to Tenterden Races in 1817. The races took place at Reading Street.

139a. & b. Two theatre posters for performances in June 1827. Oliver Goldsmith was reputed to have visited Tenterden in 1754 and played in 'Romeo and Juliet' with a band of strolling players. He described Tenterden as 'a town of taste'. The theatre itself was not built until 1794 and may have been in Theatre Square.

Last Night but ONE.

On Wednesday Evening, June the 27th, 1827, Will be presented the celebrated New MELO-DRAME (*never acted here*) entitled—THE

TWO GALLEY SLAVES.

The Unknown, Mr. HOLLAND.   Major De Lisle, Mr. WILLIAMS.
La Route, Mr. EMDEN.   Henry, Mr. MELVILLE.
Bonhomme, Mr. NEWCOMBE.   Basil, Mr. WOOLMER
Villagers, Messrs. CORK &c.
Jeannette, Miss ELLAR.   Louise, Mrs. SPILLER.

In Act 1st.---A RUSTIC DANCE by the Characters,

After which, the Comic Piece of,

LOVERS' QUARRELS.

Don Carlos, Mr. HOLLAND.   Lopez, Mr. NEWCOMBE
Sancho, Mr. WOOLMER.
Jacintha, Miss ELLAR.   Leonora, Mrs. SPILLER.

To conclude with the celebrated Romantic MELO-DRAME, entitled

VALENTINE AND ORSON

Pepin, King of France,   Mr. WILLIAMS.
Henry,   His Relations,   Mr. NEWCOMBE.
Haufray,   Mr. CORK
Valentine, the Foundling,   Mr. MELVILLE.
Hugo, his Armourer,   Mr. WOOLMER.
The Sorcerer Agramant, the Green Knight,   Mr. EMDEN.
Blandimon, Mr. HARDY. Orson, the Wild Man of the Woods, Mr. HOLLAND.
Agatha (with a Song,)   Mrs. BROOKE.
Empress Belisante, Miss ELLAR.   Princess Florimonda, Mrs. EMDEN.
And the Princess Eglantine,   Mrs. SPILLER.

The Incidents of the Piece are as follows.

Valentine and Orson, Twin Brothers, were Sons to the Empress of Greece, who was delivered of them in the Forest of Orleans: the latter was

SUCKLED BY A BEAR,

And brought up with her young. The former was found by King Pepin, as he was hunting, and brought up at that Monarch's Court, where he gained great renown by his valourous achievements, particularly when he accompanied the King in his

WARS WITH THE CARACENS;

On their return from which, the Piece Commences, with the entry of Pepin and his army into the City of Orleans, the Inhabitants of which present a Petition to the King, beseeching his aid against

A WILD MAN,

Who destroys every thing which comes within his reach, to the great annoyance of the Citizens: the vanquishing of whom is undertaken by Valentine, which he effects, after

A Dangerous Combat with the Wild Man.

He afterwards, accompanied by Orson, sets out for the Tent of Agramant, the Green Knight, to release from his power the Princess Florimonda.

A GRAND BANQUET,

At which the King is informed that his Daughter, the Princess Eglantine, has left the Palace in

THE ARMOUR OF VALENTINE.

The malicious design of Henry and Haufray to Assassinate Valentine, which is prevented by his Wild Companion: the humerous situation of Hugo, whose self-conceited valour, and his encounters with the Wild Man, tend much to enliven the Piece.

The Tent of Agramant.

The Princess Eglantine challenges the Green Knight. A broad sword Combat ensues, Eglantine is beaten down, and on the point of falling a sacrifice, but for the timely entrance of Valentine, who rescues her and challenges the Green Knight, who in derision bids him try to pull down **THE ENCHANTED SHIELD.**

Valentine persists, and encounters the Green Knight, in the conflict Valentine is overcome; Orson rushes in, and begs to fight Agramant. Valentine recollects the words of the Priest, and bids Orson try to pull away the Shield, when the Priest pronounces,

'Forbear, this Shield protects a Prince not nursed by Woman.'

The Shield flies into Orson's hand. Agramant, forewarned of his fate, rushes on Orson, but is vanquished and borne by Orson to the Palace of Ferragus, where Valentine and Orson are made acquainted with the History of their births by the mouth of

THE BRAZEN ORACLE.

The Empress of Greece is introduced to her Sons, who are both married, Valentine to Eglantine, and Orson to Florimonda.

Last Night but Three.

FOR THE BENEFIT OF

Mr. NEWCOMBE.

On Friday Evening, June the 22nd, 1827, Will be presented the celebrated and highly interesting GRAND TRAGIC DRAMA (with the original Music, and appropriate Scenery, as performed upwards of 150 nights in London entitled—

FAUSTUS

Or, The Fatal Contract.

Faustus, a German Student, by the aid of his philosophic talents, attaches to himself a Dæmon, under human form, who is named Mephistophiles, with whom he had formed an infernal compact, that for a stated period his every wish should be fulfilled; and at this period the Piece commences. The victim is gradually led from crime to crime, till the completion of the awful catastrophe. The characters are strongly drawn, the Language nervous and elegant—the Music pathetic and beautiful—and the Comic characters dispersed through the Piece, render it one of the most attractive Dramas of the modern Theatre.

Faustus, a German Student,   Mr. MELVILLE.
Mephistophiles, his attendant Dæmon,   Mr. HOLLAND.
Enrico, Brother to Adine,   Mr. EMDEN.
Wagner, Pupil to Faustus,   Mr. WOOLMER.
Count Montillo, Mr. WILLIAMS.   Count di Cassanovo, Mr. NEWCOMBE.
Lucetta, Miss ELLAR.   Countess Rosolia, Mrs. SPILLER.
Adine, the betrothed of Faustus,   Miss BROOKE.

SCENERY, &c. incidental to the Piece.

WILD and ROCKY PASS, with the

INCANTATION

And Appearance of the Dæmon!

GRAND SQUARE of NAPLES,

WITH A VIEW OF THE BAY.

A GRAND MASQUERADE.

THE PRISON OF FAUSTUS,

WITH HIS LIBERATION BY THE DÆMON.

Anti Room in the Royal Palace at Naples,

WITH THE

MURDER of the KING!

Grand Hall of Audience, with the awful Consumation!!

Distraction and Death of Adine.

THE SEIZURE OF FAUSTUS.

AWFUL APPEARANCE OF THE DÆMON!!!

THE STAGE ENVELOPED IN A LUMINOUS

RED FLAME!!

"Come, Love, to me," Grand Scena, "O Saul, O King," BY MISS BROOKE.

A COMIC SONG BY MR. NEWCOMBE.

The KING, GOD Bless Him, by Mr. WILLIAMS.

To conclude with the highly Comic Farce by Colman, of

X. Y. Z.

Or, Wanted, A Wife.

Rossius Alldross, Mr. MELVILLE. Ralph Hempseed, Mr. NEWCOMBE
Captain Galliard, Mr. WILLIAMS.   Grubbleton, Mr. HOLLAND.
Doddle, Mr. EMDEN.   Neddy Bray, Mr. WOOLMER.
Dora Mumwell, Miss ELLAR.
Maria, Mrs. SPILLER.   Mrs. Mouser, Mrs. EMDEN.

The Tenterden Band will attend.

TICKETS to be had of Mr. NEWCOMBE, at Mr. W. Dunster's

140. From 1912 residents of Tenterden were privileged to have an excellent cinema. This photograph, *c.*1935, shows members of staff, including Mr. Ron Hutchings, in uniform. In 1938 a large cinema was opened in the High Street and the original building was closed. At one time there was talk of demolishing it, but today it has been converted into shops and offices and is known as The Fairings.

141. Miss Margaret Babington, daughter of the Rev. John Babington who was vicar of St Mildred's parish church 1907-24, organised a number of entertainments over the years. On 11 and 12 July 1911 the church held a fête and one of the most popular items was a waxworks tableau in which many local people took part.

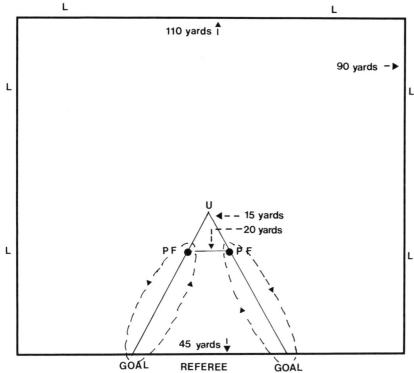

Key: **L** = Linesmen (6); **U** = Umpires (2); **PF** = Point Flag

142a. Tenterden goal running
team in action on the local
ground, *c*.1920. The team,
comprising 22 players,
belonged to the Romney Marsh
and District Goal Running
League. The aim of each player
was either to touch an
opponent, scoring a 'stroke', or
to run around his opponent's
point flag, scoring a 'point'. The
main objective of the game was
to keep the point flag well
protected and for players to
follow one another in close
succession; a player can only
escape by running to a
boundary line. When a player
scores a stroke he 'whoops' and
all players return to base and
start again. A penalty is
awarded if a player whoops
without touching his man.

142b. Plan of a goal running
playing field based on one of the
few published pitch plans, from
the *Kentish Express* 16 July 1921.
From the mid-1850s to the
1930s there were between 80
and 100 goal running clubs in
Kent.

EVENTS

143.   Queen Victoria's Diamond Jubilee was celebrated with a party in the High Street, 1897.

144. This 'Welcome' took place outside the Town Hall in 1901 when Private Albert Millen (on the right in the coach) and Private Arthur George Watson, members of G. Coy. 2nd Vol. Batt. East Kent Regiment (the Buffs) returned from fighting in the Boer War. These local heroes were welcomed by the Mayor (Mr. E. H. Hardcastle) and Corporation. Privates Millen and Watson were pulled in triumph in the decorated mayor's carriage through the streets of Tenterden by members of the local fire brigade. They were presented with a silver keyless watch each together with a sum of money; 300 residents had contributed towards this. Private Millen, amid loud cheering, ascended the platform and returned thanks for the kind reception given to him and his colleague.

145. The proclamation of King George V took place outside the Town Hall on 9 May 1910. The Mayor, Mr. E. Apps, is wearing his chain of office. Also in the picture are the Vicar, the Town Clerk in wig and gown, behind him J. Ellis Mace J.P., various Aldermen and Councillors, and the Clerk of the Peace (again in wig and gown). To the left of the archway is the vine-covered *Woolpack Inn*.

146. Waterloo Day at Tenterden, *c.*1910. Heading the procession are members of the fire brigade, followed by the town band, then a group of children and a contingent from the Buffs, the Royal East Kent Regiment, in which many local boys served.

147. Bazaar at Hales Place, 1911. The house built in the 15th century was the seat of the Hales family; John Hales became the first Mayor of Tenterden. Part of the Tudor mansion was demolished in the 18th century, including the banqueting hall. The house ceased to be occupied by the family in 1893. Among those present in the picture are the Vicar, the Rev. John Babington, who served the town from 1907-24, his daughter Miss Margaret Babington, E. H. Hardcastle, Lady Mabel Egerton and Earl Brassey.

148. Funeral procession of Admiral Sir Charles Drury, who died while Mayor of Tenterden in 1914. The bier was pulled by a contingent of Sea Cadets as befitted a man who had spent over 52 years in the Royal Navy, which he had joined when only 12 years of age. The local dignitaries are here preceded by the two mace-bearers, passing in front of the *White Lion Hotel*; the maids in their white aprons are watching from a carriage archway. The cottages on the right have now been demolished.

149a. & b.   Two photographs of the funeral of Admiral Sir Charles Drury on 22 May 1914.

150. Homewood House at the time it was inhabited by Admiral Sir Charles and Lady Drury, *c.*1912. The Admiral bought the house in 1910 and altered it considerably, enlarging the two side wings. He died in 1914 but his widow continued to reside there until 1947 when she sold the house to Kent County Council, together with 50 acres, for £10,000. The building subsequently became part of Homewood Comprehensive School.

151. Bert Milsted, Ted Jenner and Harry Brunger with the first wireless set in Tenterden, seen here at the Town Hall. Unfortunately, it has been impossible to date this photograph.

152. After World War One, war memorials were set up in small villages and churchyards throughout the country. This picture of the unveiling of the plaque at Ebony Church on 22 July 1920 shows the surrounding marshland and grazing sheep. It is believed that this church was moved from the original island of Ebony to the hamlet of Reading Street which is within the boundaries of the old borough of Tenterden.

153. Before World War Two, children always celebrated Empire Day on 24 May. In Tenterden they assembled on the recreation ground, many of them carrying Union flags, and paraded before local dignitaries. They were normally given a half-day holiday and sometimes a small gift. This photograph shows Empire Day celebrations in 1921.

ST MICHAELS

154. Both Tenterden and its suburb of St Michaels, formerly known as Boresisle, were completely rural until well into this century, as seen in this *c*.1910 photograph.

155. Old Cottages at St Michaels early this century, before the extensive building programme took place.

156. St Michael's church school was built in 1863 and for a time it served as a place of worship for this part of Tenterden; the church itself was completed a few months later. Dedicated to St Michael and All Angels, it gave its name to this area which was formerly known as Boresisle or Birdsisle. The steeple, now a landmark in the surrounding countryside, was not completed until 12 years after the consecration of the church, the cost being met by voluntary contributions. This photograph was taken at the turn of the century.

157. Cottages and church of St Michaels from a sketch by X. Willis, 1902.

158.   Members of the Cottingham family outside the forge in Ashford Road, St Michaels, *c*.1935.

159. An old cottage at Smallhythe early in the present century. Arthur Chacksfield ran a shop from the small shed next door.

SMALLHYTHE FROM THE TOLL GATE.

160. The tollgate at Smallhythe, *c.*1900, looking northwards. This sketch first appeared in volume IV of a series of books called *A Saunter Through Kent with Pen and Pencil* written by Charles Igglesden and illustrated by X. Willis. Sir Charles was an author and journalist and for many years editor of the *Kentish Express*. Unfortunately, nothing is known about the artist who accompanied him on his travels throughout the county between 1900 and 1930.

161. An early photograph of the tollgate at Smallhythe, with Ellen Terry's cottage on the right.

162. Smallhythe was originally the port for Tenterden and shipped cargoes of wool and other goods to the continent. It is still possible to trace a slip repair dock. The river was navigable for barges until the present century. This photograph was taken *c.*1900.

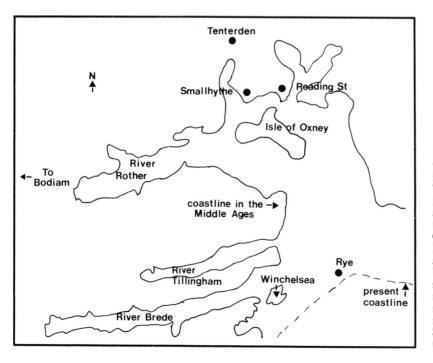

163. Conjectural map of the coastline when Tenterden was at the height of its prosperity during the Middle Ages. The river ports of Smallhythe and Reading Street were on a northern arm of the river Rother which at this time was navigable as far as Bodiam Castle, built by Sir Edward Dallingrigge as a defence post against attacking French raiders. Old Winchelsea was destroyed by the great storm of 1287 and the Isle of Oxney is now a hillock in the surrounding marshlands. Boats were able to navigate the river Rother as far as Smallhythe during the early years of this century.

164. Today Smallhythe is a quiet backwater rather than a thriving port. The church of St John the Baptist seen in this picture was rebuilt in 1516/17 and replaced an earlier one which was burnt down with most of the hamlet in 1514.

165. The small thatched cottage which once stood beside the church of St John the Baptist was burnt down in 1910.

166. Priest's House, Smallhythe, in 1890. The road leads to Romney Marsh and in the distance is the tollgate. This property is now under National Trust ownership.

167. Smallhythe Place, now owned by the National Trust, was once the home of the famous actress Dame Ellen Terry who purchased the property in 1899 and lived there until her death in 1928. It now houses a display of theatrical memorabilia. Originally a half-timbered yeoman's house, it dates from 1480 and was at one time the residence of the Port Officer.

168.   Dame Ellen Terry lived at Smallhythe Place for 29 years until her death in 1928. She was born at Coventry in 1848 and for a number of years lived in Tower Cottage in Winchelsea where she was known for her good works; at one point she was reputed to have shod every child in the town. Dame Ellen made her first public appearance at the Princess's Theatre in 1856 where she was Mamillius in 'A Winters Tale', under the direction of Charles Kean. Her association with Sir Henry Irving commenced in about 1870 and their friendship remained unbroken until the beginning of this century. Ellen Terry's first husband was G. F. Watts, a well-known artist of the period, who painted her as a girl with flowing pre-Raphaelite hair early in their marriage. This photograph was taken around 1920.

Bibliography

Archaeologia Cantiana Vols. 32 & 33, articles by A. H. Taylor

Bignell, Alan, *Kent Lore a Heritage of Fact and Fable* (1983)

Burke, Thomas, *The Beauty of England* (1933)

Bushell, T. A., *Barracuda Guide to Kent* (Chesham, 1976)

Finch, William Coles, *Watermills and Windmills* (1933)

Glover, Judith, *The Place Names of Kent* (1975)

Guide to Ellen Terry Museum

Guide to the Parish Church of St Mildred

Harvey Darton, F. J., *A Parcel of Kent* (1924)

Hatcher, Dorothy, *The Workhouse and the Weald* (Rainham, 1988)

Igglesden, Charles, *A Saunter Through Kent with Pen and Pencil Vol.lV*, Illustrated by X. Willis (Ashford, 1902)

Kent Archaeological Society Vol. XX (Chichester, 1971)

Mace, J. Ellis, J.P., *Tenterden Old & New* (Tenterden, 1902)

Maxwell, Donald, *Unknown Kent* (1921)

Murray, Walter J. C., *Romney Marsh* (Bath, 1970)

Newman, John, *West Kent & The Weald* (1969)

Spelling, R. S., *Tenterden* (Rochester, 1985)

Tenterden Town Guide (1972-3)

Winstanley, Michael, *Life in Kent at the Turn of the Century* (Folkestone, 1978)